EIGHT SENSES PLUS TWO

CAMELIA ELIAS

EIGHT SENSES PLUS TWO

EYECORNER PRESS

Published by EYECORNER PRESS 2008

© Camelia Elias 2008

All rights reserved. Printed in the US and UK.

ISBN: 978-87-992456-1-1

Most of the poems in Part I have been published as a limited artprint under the title *Eight Senses Plus One*.

Cover design:
after a collograph print by Ann Kerstina Nielsen
www.ann-kerstina.dk

For Bent Sørensen

ACKNOWLEDGEMENT

The author wishes to thank all those whom she
mentions, dead or alive, and whom she knows
– so help her God –
for their generosity.
They will have allowed her to ambush them.

What better entertaining, she is thinking to herself,
unless, there is more?

CONTENTS

Husbands and Wives / 13
Scholars of Habits / 15
Unisons / 16
Pop-Up Books / 17
Lucky Numbers / 18
Hermes in a Nutshell / 19
Gas / 20
Autograph / 25
Musketeer Logic / 26
Stone Slabs / 27
Tele-visions / 29
Qurious / 31
Queering the Pitch / 33
Marginally Yours / 35
Wonderlands / 37
Bifurcation Theory / 38
Seduction / 40
Magister Ludi / 42
In Praise of Pandemonium / 47
Communal Love / 49
Checkmate / 51
If I ever / 53
"That's when you fall" / 55
Das Kapital / 57
Plutocrats / 58
Sisyphus Time / 60
"Where'er we Tread 'Tis Haunted Holy Ground" / 62
The H Fugue / 64

About the Author / 67

I
~~~

Talking about one's self is a feast that starves the guest.

– Guy Davenport

He says: "all you need is love."
She says: "really?"

HUSBANDS AND WIVES

THE year is 2003 and I decide to give my husband a calendar. One of those that offer an aphorism a day. My idea is to supplement others' wisdom with my own, prompted by my husband's body. His body smells of writing. Every morning. Among other smells. And I've been meaning to translate his smell into articulation. For some time now. So he gets his calendar, and the first entry I write is this one: "green colors under the bed." There is no aphorism to go with this line. The calendar offers a rebus instead. When the editors run out of aphorisms, they put a crossword puzzle instead. I read the clues. They are all in Danish: *gro sammen*, grow together, *eksisterer*, exists, *ordentlig*, decent, though this last one can also have other meanings, depending on context. "Right," I say. "I can't use that for anything. Besides, I've always been bad at puzzles." It's frustrating to declare your words beat by numbers. X-Locutio eloquence.

THE year is 2008. My husband is 50. I search through the 2003 calendar entries and while reading and getting amused at my silly associations, it occurs to me that the line quoted above, the one that has green colors under the bed in it, was written in connection with a dream. I had dreamt that I washed Jacques Derrida's feet. The way Pentecostals do it. We are not Pentecostals, but I have secretly attended some of these rituals, so I know what they mean when they do it. But something escapes me. I put the unknown, the X, in an equation. I should tell my husband that I want to write like Gertrude Stein, or like Lynn Emanuel on Gertrude Stein, or on herself for that matter. Gertrude said that the letter X is funny and that everybody knows that, and that X itself knows that. She was such a literalist. I like to know when my husband is funny. It's the only duty as a wife that I can stand.

SCHOLARS OF HABITS

WE are moving to a place with no bathtub. This is a disaster. My husband tries to comfort me. "The windows are big so we can bathe in the sunset, or in the sunrise. Whichever we prefer." But I think of fabrics. Lush towels pregnant with visions. I ask: "is it a silk sunset?" "No," he says. "Is it a cashmere sunrise?" "No," he says. "The windows are a bathtub of literary skills, so the rising and the setting can be modified according to whichever texture we prefer." I touch a window and it is cold. We'll need to stuff a goat in it.

UNISON

"BACH had all these children," I say to him. "My God. Listen." I hear myself chant the Lord's prayer according to myself: "God forbid. God save me from the trouble. God save the Queen, myself, that is. God have mercy." Bach is pumping the organ. Fat sounds pour into my feminism. I melt, so I decide to develop an interest in cloning. It occurs to me that cloning sounds a bit like loony baloney. My husband says, quoting John Lennon: "all you need is love." "It's a good beginning," I say. "The letter L has just cloned itself." Accompanied by Bach it turns into a (singing) number. More. Or less.

POP-UP BOOKS

I tell my husband that I don't want to write children's books. Just because I see him floating again, now in a blimp, now in a balloon. "But children would like to hear about such things," he says. But I'm not thinking of children. I'm thinking of mothers whose sons have grown up to be round. I want to say to them: "that was a good round you gave there. You've rounded it up quite well." My husband is well-rounded. I ask him about that. Make the unpardonable advance: "was it your mother?" I smell a social determinist answer. But he goes the Nietzschean way: he tells me that roundness of character, full bodied roundness, is a matter of a will to perceive. He never saw his father take out the trash, so he resolved for the future to wrap it up himself instead of waiting for the other to do it. This almost makes me pop the question – we are not really married – but then I think of Marx. He wins.

LUCKY NUMBERS

I never use the phrase: "the truth is." Though I say it all the time, only, in other words, or numbers, as the case is more often. First of all, second of all, third of all. "Do numbers represent us?" "Yes, they do," he says. "I like to count the stars," he furthermore says. "The truth is," he says again, "I wanted to become an astronomer when I grew up." "Oh, why didn't you?" I ask. "I've always wanted to marry an astrophysicist." "Astronomer," he corrects me. "There is a difference." Just my luck. I can't even tell these things apart. I wanted to be a judge when I grew up. When I did grow up I still wanted to be judge. First of all there is evidence. Second of all there is evidence. Third of all there is evidence. I'm good at telling the first apart from the second and the second apart from the third. I interpret the wording of things, not the words themselves. I triangulate the physics of my astral hours. "To judge yourself is to stand against distinctions," he says. I'm thinking of the phrase "drawn and quartered." I've stopped desiring judging. My writing betrays my high treason.

HERMES IN A NUTSHELL

EVERY morning I ask the question: "do you know a secret?" I'm ready to enact my domestic role. At 8 o'clock I'm the secretary of gnomic affairs. "Tell me," he says. "Today you are a peach orchard in a floating bubble," I say. "Fair enough," he says. He believes me. At 8 o'clock he is in charge of opening the safety-box where our balloon language is kept over night.

GAS

WE are sitting in the sofa, my husband and I, in our Arne Norell sofa, with our laptops on small round tables, our Kasper Salto *Little Friend* tables that can be elevated or lowered by what the Danes call a *gaspatron*. I'm managing my friends on *Myspace*, *Facebook*, and *hi5*; first the dead ones, then the real ones, then the ethnic ones. My husband tells me that he has just posted a message that contains a quote. He knows I'm into quotes. So I read it quickly: "Beware of thinkers whose minds function only when they are fueled by a quotation." I make a note of Cioran's words of wisdom for later use. I like to quote Cioran. I use him all the time especially as fuel for my puns. I like to pun, though my English is not always up to it, as a critic once said. But puns should not be up to aptitudes – I think of Shakespeare. I'm attracted to Cioran because he is the least punning writer of aphorisms. When he shoots through carefully crafted formulations his caliber leaves a smell of scented gas; gas that smells of laminate. Words skate on the surface, and I wonder if a pun would not be better penned down by ink than ether.

In actual fact, the female function is to explore, discover, invent, solve problems, crack jokes, make music – all with love. In other words, create a magic world.

– Valerie Solanas

She says: "the difference between men and women is a historical one."
They say: "really?"

AUTOGRAPH

For Jacques Derrida

I told him what Derrida said, that there is no such thing as a fragment. I told him that whenever Derrida saw me, however, he would ask nevertheless: are there any fragments in it? I knew why Derrida asked me that. Because he thought that the fragment which *is not* is a sensuous thing. That I never argued with. Now we make fun of Derrida's serious interest and desire to know more about the sexual life of philosophers. I want to sign myself over to that thought. To be or not to be a philosopher. That is the question. Live and tell. "Are we going to go naked now?" he asks, signing himself over to living. I tell him to wait. I have to think about it.

MUSKETEER LOGIC

For Raymond Federman

BETWEEN us, giving and taking is a relative matter. Precisely. Einstein said to make things as simple as possible, but not any simpler. On precision he couldn't have put it more relatively. All precision that has to do with measuring how much we give and how much we take is relative. "Yes," he says, "musketeers were very good at figuring that one out, but only when they were dressed androgynously." "What's that supposed to mean?" I ask, feeling offended for having the picture of my heroes ruined. I expect him to say "nothing," but instead he says, "double and everything," paraphrasing a modern musketeer. Raymond Federman's American book, *Double or Nothing*, which is more of a fragment of a paradox – a French book dressed in Jewish clothes – is all about measuring giving and taking. What bothers me is the "everything". Relativity in androgynous dress has a special kind of gravitas. Not every matter of simplicity is simple. Some are chosen to be complex.

STONE SLABS

For Michael Riffaterre

MY husband hates the French. I can't figure out why. But then I go to New York to meet an old man of French letters – the last academic aristocrat some would claim. We talk about fragments and other riffraff. It goes with his name: Riffaterre. He wants me to be down to earth and present him with concrete problems. I think of Rimbaud's metaphysics. Then Riffaterre goes: "I wish that all metaphysicians would be hanged." I feel trapped between Riffaterre's hexagonal slabs – by the way, 19th century French literature is full of slabs – and my husband's baloney approval of Riffaterre's views. Deliriously I begin to see hanged men everywhere. Fortunately, my schooling saves me. I was a diligent student of French realist novels, or rather, romance novels. So when I come to the musketeers I take a deep breath. Their swords ease the tension between the cardinal's wit and the legendary *carte blanche*. The rings fall into the glass. Champagne is never mentioned in these novels. I wonder what Riffaterre would make of that if he were still alive. But he lies under one of his slabs. In New York he didn't want to teach me literature. He spoke of castles, moonlight, and ghosts. He told me I was fearless. My husband endorses that view too. I drink some champagne and think of my stone. It's round. And the epitaph reads: "She said... and she was right." Now I'm tempted to say: "death is the simplest of events, but it has generated the most complex cultural matrix." More slabs, actually. I wonder if I should continue drinking – to that.

TELE-VISIONS

For Søren Hattesen Balle

"WERE you on the phone again? I tried calling you," he says. The temporal adverb doesn't refer to time but to my best friend. He's the only one I ever speak with on the phone. For hours. "Yes," I say. "It's Wittgenstein again". The temporal adverb doesn't refer to time but to my husband's anticipated reaction. "It figures," he says. He hates philosophers, but because Wittgenstein is a formalist he manages to make it in the crowd of few who are not dismissed. "How about bedsheets?" he asks. He wants to know whether I've informed my friend of my new purchase – white damask by Geismar. My bedsheets are always white, and my friend is the only one on this planet who knows that I get neurotic if I sleep in color. I think of Wittgenstein. He liked to do his friends' dishes in a bathtub. Same thing really. White dishes through white water made so by white enamel. Then I think of Lou Salomé. What a gay *ménage à trois* with Nietzsche and Paul Rée. I wonder who did the shopping. My friend knows that if conventions didn't dictate *passo doble*, we would all be *trio-ing* about. Just like that. Very colorfully. But we are not that mad, or suicidal, or gay. We teleport our thoughts along our steps, not into them. Dust on our shoes. We sleep with ghosts and do their plates. Wittgenstein just dropped a knife. The sound cuts through water. Starched formalism divided. We wrap our thoughts and go to the movies.

QURIOUS

For Vincent F. Hendricks

IT starts with charting the symmetrical relation of curiosity to desire. Curiosity is articulated. Desire is not. Desire is X. We play the game of who gets the X faster. I want to win. He wants to win. Grammar of seduction. I win the first round, because I bring in Tiresias – of whom he knows nothing – thus avoiding making trivial remarks on the life and times of curious cats. I tease desire out of its skull. The mind still wants to know the unknown. The first statement falls: "I won't come tonight, unless you insist" – I don't insist. I invent a scenario and run it through a probability test. I want to stake a winning bet, so I say: "insofar as you would have wanted me to insist for you to come, you would thus have come, but not because I insisted but because you wanted to." All statements in this formulation are true, so I'm happy with this picture. He is not. He grants me winning over the X, but calls my logic demented. I put on my favorite cape, the judicial one, and ask: "Please answer the question: upon having been summoned, and after having come as a consequence of having been summoned, would you, or would you not have come because you wanted to?" He says, "I would have." It's his turn to win the X, but then he makes the mistake of getting into details: "but I would also have come for other reasons too: to give you the book, the quotes, see your face, hear you think." As a judge, being summoned to preside over symmetries I'm bound to dismiss the new evidence on account of precedence. Tiresias didn't end so well. He created too much narrative, as a man, and as a woman. "We must keep it simple," I say. Our questions must follow a vital call to Eros: who wants what from whom must stop after the pronoun. I get rid of catharsis and occupy the stark and liminal space of abstraction. He follows, but only because he is curious. This time I believe him, so he wins. But the X casts a spell on our naked speech, and neither of us wins.

QUEERING THE PITCH

For Hartmut Haberland

I throw one word at him. He throws three back. It's a fair move. He is the master and I learn. "Give me something on *prophet*," I say. He makes a circular move, takes a bow, identifies himself with his name, and enumerates his titles: "an omnivorous, abominable, but far from omniscient omnibus punster." Then he quotes Freud who said "Anatomie ist das Schicksal". I pull a Danish face and throw it into his German: "Hva' be' ha'? The land where words hibernate?" Ich habe ein heartfelt concern. "No, I don't feel like a prophet," I reply, to his "why" question. "I become," I say. I get academic and explain in a pedestrian manner: "the prophetic is inherent in the process of prophesying. It means *becoming*. This however creates an interesting tension where symmetry is concerned: a prophesy implies something that will have come (quite ominously), pointing to a final point of no return; *becoming* remains forever in a developing state, a potential *being* that awaits actualization." "Yes, yes, but where is the fun in that," he wants to know. "No fun," I say, "prophets are not in the business of imitating Italians on the phone:

pronto?" My mother was a Marxist who liked prophets, because their names start with the letter S: schmucks, schnoorers, schmekers. "Hoola baloola," he says, pointing to prophets' getting high in highlands not their own. "I know, it's hysterical," I say. "All that harababura for nicht gesundheit."

MARGINALLY YOURS

For Lynn Emanuel

HE thinks I should write more on David Markson. My specialty is male authors, except for Gertrude Stein. But I leave it to Lynn to handle it. Her typewriter is better than mine. And she knows the inside of Gertrude. "It is dark in there," the other Lynn says. She separates my interest for periods with a comma borrowed from Gertrude. Gertrude, as we all know was a master at repeating, and saved loads of punctuation for critics to come. I used to be into tormented modernists. Except Eliot. I leave that to Søren. He has infinite patience. I don't. Today modernists get the ax, my ax. Except Celan. I rest my case where the others are concerned. The judge is happy that we waste no time, so the verdict can fall: dismissed, dismissed, dismissed, dead, dead, dead. Enters Markson. Needless to say, his *Wittgenstein's Mistress* is Markson's specialty where woman is concerned. But he leaves it to her to choose living with men in pictures. She then leaves it to the pictures to make it perfect. Lynn knows a thing or two about pictures. She showed me when we were standing in front of the *Book of Letters* in Libeskind's museum. We make fun of Wittgenstein in Markson's other novel, *This is not a Novel*. Says he: "Among Wittgenstein's spelling when using English: Anoied. Realy. Excelentely. Expences. Affraid. Cann't." Lynn and I can spell. Also backwards. Picture perfect.

"HELLO!" he yells from refraction. "I said, you should write on Markson." But Lynn and I are watching Wittgenstein, who, "like a patient etherized upon a table," rocks the proof.

WONDERLANDS

For Charles Lock

"WHERE do we go from here?" he asks. "Do we have to?" I reply. I like the *aca-nada*, nothing here, if I can write it myself in that *u-topic*, no place, place. He is thinking about it. He is looking for a punch-line. No one writes better punch-lines. And then it comes: "If you have to write *nothing*, do it with your lips. Let the air pass through, and mimic the words as you would write them with your eyes, and then think of a clown. "Sure," I say, "that's easy." I see myself already vanishing through his ears.

BIFURCATION THEORY

For Alex Nicolin

"IN physics a horseshoe is more than a symbol for luck; it's a matter of trust," I tell him. Bohr didn't believe that luck stepped in in flat iron heels, but he believed the person who said to him that whether he believed it or not, it was true. This is what I would call a ratio of convergence, though Feigenbaum might disagree. "Are you going to hang out with the nerds again?", he wants to know. He heard me mumbling to myself: "epsilon over square root of gamma," "X is in the rescaled deviation from the equilibrium width." "Yes," "I need to calculate precisely how much I'm going to excite the first resonance." He knows that this is what I do when I go in the negative: no understanding, no knowledge, no vision, no priming of the reader, no spreading of atomic legs, no horseshit, no certain energies, no bouncing.

I apply some Bohrian psychoanalysis to myself: g forces, horses, and spots set the shape of the function of narrative. Bohr is exasperated: you're mixing the gs with the qs again. Stick with Gauss. But I'm already in a Bose trance.

Condensed thinking is cold thinking. I lose my individual identity. My blob coalesces with exotic geometries. No one understands a thing, but it is beautiful. Blip.

SEDUCTION

"WHAT does it mean to seduce people?" he asks, and he never asks philosophical questions. She needs to be fast, she thinks. By God, the opportunity is here to finally win him over to the abstract side. But she is goddamned smart and knows already that that *ain't gonna happen*, ever. She pretends she doesn't know this already; she should have been a psychoanalyst, as she likes to manipulate people, as she always knows what they are thinking, as she knows exactly what seduction is. He knows this too. Where she is concerned, "when intuition and logic agree, she is always right." And so she is. She says, donning a Transylvanian accent: "seduction, seduction, seduction, well now, let's see. This is diiiiffffiiicult. This is cooomplexxx." She adopts a peripatetic posture, and simulates a contemporary management policy: "I don't know, what do you think? You seduced me once." This he denies vehemently. He throws the evidence at her, which she knows already he would, as he is equally goddamned smart, and says: "there was writing; your writing. You coerced me into replying, and ever since then I've been writing for you." She knows this, and she is flattered. But she chooses to say, "yes, yes, there was writing, but if you must know, it was the smell that did it." He looks at her incredulously, but then she argues, being perfectly conscious of the circumstantial fallacy of relevance: "it's not my fault that you can't smell your own body." He would like to know what it is that she can smell, but all she has to say, without answering his question, is this: "seduction is a foot without a shoe in winter." She is lying.

MAGISTER LUDI

For Camelia Elias

BENT says: are you finished with your abstractions?
Søren says: if the Queens wants it, she can have it.
Vincent says: what's in it for us?
Hartmut says: why me?
Charles says: can we have more puns?
Lynn says: is the book done?
Alex says: meson or Masonic?
Raymond says: quite a woman and quite a scholar.
Jacques says: I'm tired of imbeciles, can we do a chiasmus?
Michael says: let us go now, you and I, and hang some philosophers.
Camelia says: this is abso-fucking-lutely brilliant!

III
~~~

Der Tod ist ein Meister.

– Paul Celan

She says: "the Germans had a thing for truth and death."
He says: "really?"

IN PRAISE OF PANDEMONIUM

For Hamlet

HE said: "To be or not to be, that is the question." I'm tired after moving, which involved reading all the books again before putting them on the shelves. The Shakespeare – all works in one – book is sticking out, and I'm tired of thinking of that one line. "Why can't I think of another," I ask myself? I'm tired of dying people asking questions. Gertrude asked Alice: "what is the answer?" and when Alice didn't say anything, she said, "in that case, what is the question?" At least Gertrude was smart and didn't procrastinate her own death for a philosophical question. My books have arranged themselves while I closed my eyes and thought of England. Agamben should come before Artaud in the alphabetical order. But I don't want to ask myself whether I should follow the compulsion to letter or not. I reason that since Artaud kept it simple, he should get the honor of beginning theory. *Here then the Question* is the first book on my first theory shelf. After Derrida, who makes it in the first round, the first shelf ends with Leslie Fiedler's *Waiting for the End*. "This shelf means serious business," I tell myself. "I need a break,"

I tell myself again. Hamlet follows, and I ask him whether he wouldn't mind laying it off. I don't want to be fucked in the middle of putting things together. From my vantage point I see the paperback section. Some tall books stick out, and I'm happy to procrastinate helping Hamlet out. The titles that I can read are these: *Re-search* (Burroughs), Elias (Canetti), *The Woman who is the Midnight*, (Terence Green) *The Greek Way* (Edith Hamilton) *Scratching* (*The Beat Surface*, McClure), *Tropic of Capricorn* (Miller). "Woa, this is even more serious," I tell myself. What's eating Miller, after all that sex with Anaïs Nin? His first was *Tropic of Cancer*. Gertrude died of cancer to her stomach. "That's it," I say, and yell to Hamlet: "Hamlet, fuck philosophy! Off we go." He's happy to procrastinate, yet again. We want our books to be crazy about us, just the way we're crazy about them. Their authors? (Here then the question) – we don't mind them dead. *Fin*, as they say in French movies. *Finitto*, in Italian. *Tutti morti*, if you want to dramatize. The other Gertrude, Hamlet's mother, has nothing to say.

COMMUNAL LOVE

For Alfred

HE comes home and tells me while cracking up: "J. Alfred Prufrock's meanderings from brothel to brothel have been turned into a theme of love and community." "Really?", I say. "That's interesting. Who has been over interpreting?", I furthermore inquire. "Evidently not students," he says. "They usually either get it or they don't." I feel like a student. "It's a teacher in high school," he says. "Oh," I say, and lose interest. I'm more into the notion of *dasein*, being among the women. It helped Michelangelo in Dante's *Inferno* to be gay. But Eliot didn't get it, and that's why his Alfred got etherized. All men who think they are straight but in reality are not pose questions. Alfred drives me nuts: "What is it?", "Do I dare, do I dare?", "Disturb the universe?", "And how should I presume?", "And how should I begin?" "And should I then presume?" "For Christ's sake," I think. "I'm not even in Norway yet, where climbing walls is a piece of cake." Give me Seneca as a woman. But Greek philosophers don't lend themselves so easily to feminization. It's easier with the Latin ones. All you need to do is replace the consonantal *us* at the end of their names with the vowels *ia*. Marcus Aurelius, Marcia Aurelia. "Lazarus, Lazarus," Prufrock yells in awe of the *geist* upright, uptight, and properly resurrected. But he is of course thinking of Lazara.

IN Michael Hollinger's new play *Opus* Elliot is a lead intellectual in the fictional but famous Lazara Quartet. The other Eliot was into *Quartets*. Quarter this and quarter that. Divide by four and love thy community. After love making, Prufrock is now into making name tags. Catherine Gonnard and Elisabeth Lebovici are supervising: "Jacqueline Pollock, Marcelle Duchamp, Miss van der Rohe, Francine Picabia, Renée Magritte." There are no unknowns here. It is clear that two plus two is five.

CHECKMATE

For Moinuous and Namredef

OLA, ola, ola, bola, bola, bola. This is not exactly *Parsifal*. Moinous and Namredef like Parsifal. After a lot of singing, there is a lot of dying. "I don't want to go to Dachau," I tell them. I just want the singing. Namredef blurts at me and almost tells me to go fuck myself. "Don't get so worked up," he says, "I'm Jewish too, you know," he further says. "Ya, sure," I say, and start thinking about what would have happened to Malcolm X's philosophy had he gone to Europe to visit the old concentration camps instead of Mecca. I'm getting twofold vibrations. I wonder if Federman's family had a brief encounter with Max Ernst and Peggy Guggenheim while in there, at that place, the place that Wagner never wanted to mention. Peggy and Max got out. Then Max married Peggy and then he married that American who still wants a lot of colors in her dreams. I see them playing chess in one of Inverarity's framed photographs. Malcolm said: "Be peaceful, be courteous, obey the law, respect everyone;

but if someone puts his hand on you, send him to the cemetery." Moinous and Namredef understand this very well, but only when pronounced in another language. They love their reactions to such statements to end with *Halleluiah* and *Amen*, but since they are more cultivated than most Baptists, they like an ending that goes Latin. Thus their favorite is: *nec plus ultra*. Oy, boy! Before the King goes into checkmate, the Queen gives him a kiss under their gazes. M & N approve.

IF I EVER

For Tiresias

"STOP reading signs. Sense them," he tells me. "Stop reading altogether," he furthermore says. I'm happy to oblige. I've just been on the phone with Georg Cantor and he told me the same thing. I presented Cantor with a line from Shakespeare's King Lear: "never, never, never, never, never." Shakespeare knew his Sophocles. Cantor didn't. Cantor knew set theory, but Tiresias beat him to it. "Infinity is a question of trust," I imagine Cantor saying. I believe him. There is a reason why Lear said what he said five times. Tiresias prophesized twice as a woman, twice as a man, and once as a sex god for good measure. Blindness is knowledge that can't tolerate one's knowing that one sees.

NOTHING converges with never. Not even when we insist five times. I vacillate between the trivial and the momentous. The Greek choir that numbers the fabulous five: Cantor, Lear, Tiresias, Shakespeare, and Sophocles, urges me on: "forget about the whole thing, but don't forget us."

I nod. Everything is possible in the infinite. No chaste divas are allowed there. Only fractions. And fractals. And fragments.

THAT'S WHEN YOU FALL

For Madame George

THIS opera and that opera, this Schubert and that Schubert, this drama and that drama. This is all my ranting. He's trying to get a word in. "Yes, but how about Bob Dylan?" "Who?" I say. "Never heard of him. Or wait." I'm having an epiphany. "Yes, yes, of course, isn't he the one who's banging on that instrument that is so deafening?" "Sorry," I say, "except for Wagner, I don't like loud and disconcerting music." "Fair enough," he says, laughing at such embodied ignorance. He has seen better days and women. He decides to go for Van the Man. He doesn't answer either to the Irish or the English stereotype of the man of the day. Larkin has both the priest and the doctor running around in their long coats over the field after having solved the puzzle of what a day is good for in this life. Van laments: "Oh, won't you stay, Stay a while with your own ones, Don't ever stray, Stray so far from your own ones." Van is into astral weeks not days. Some formal introduction is needed, we all feel. "Madame George, Camelia Elias, Camelia Elias, Madame George." "Elias is from Vienna, a good acquaintance of Stefan Zweig," he says. La George bows. She knows Zweig's work on astral hours. And Elias is totally into prophets. "Let's go see one," she says. But as she doesn't like the train, she suggests that they all take the plane and fly to Israel. Elias needs to see her mother before the fall. The other two have businesses of their own.

DAS KAPITAL

For Billy Pilgrim

"STOP stepping on my toes." He says this the second I'm about to go: "Wow, you have such warm toes." "I'm looking for the plunger," I say, and I can already see the answer coming: "well, it's not between my toes." "Too bad," I think to myself. That would have been interesting. My husband kidnapped by the Tralfamadorians who urge him to make the pilgrimage to Dollywood. They can't figure out what's wrong with Billy and the Blondie. My husband goes: "in Dollywood, the 'never mind' replaces 'so it goes.' I myself was 'in the meanwhile' when the plunger sucked me into the defeatist discourse: stepped on toes or stabbed toes? He wants to know what I need the plunger for. "Nothing," I say, "I just want it next to my favorite picture of a man of style." "Karl Kapital" the caption says, referring to a good soldier who refuses to die. No 'so it goes' there. Lagerfeld in his library: 300000 books. I'm ready to swoon over so many zeroes. I dream of getting myself published by 7L. In French this goes like *Cette Elle*: This she. *C'est elle*: It's her. Pink dolls have no toes. So it goes.

PLUTOCRATS

For Senator Pat Geary

THE Godfather has heard that I'm good at staging plays. So he calls me up. He wants the exchanges between the Senator and Michael to be pepped up. "Me," I ask? "Ok, no problem." After all, I have been in Marthaler's school, and I paid attention, so I hurry to offer an instant solution. You can't be kidding with the MOB. "Here's what we do," I say. "We have to have these guys end their quarrel on a friendly note. We need to think especially of the senator." Vito Corleone says in the background: "make him an offer he can't refuse." LOL. "That's right" I say, "so where were we?" "Yes, we start with the senator, as he is baffled." WTF? So he says: "I'm a blunt man, and I intend to speak very frankly to you, perhaps more frankly than any has ever done before". OMG, this sounds ominous, but Michael knows what he is doing. He says: "Senator? You can have my answer now, if you like. My final offer is this: nothing. Not even the fee for the gaming license, which I would appreciate if you would put up personally." I direct: "good tone, Michael, but try to be more suggestive of your belonging, you know, show that you are a real MOT. I glance at the Godfather and he is restless. He yells: "F a duck! Does this have anything to do with that Modal Operator T? We don't want any logic here. We want emotion." SBJ, now I'm really afraid. But a genuine MOT comes to my rescue. Hyman Roth intervenes: "What I am saying is, we have now what we have always needed, real partnership with the government." S.S.X. The Godfather is pleased with the new play. "So the name won't be tainted? Can we dedicate all these guns to ourselves?" "Yes," I say. "No water pistols. Promise. Real guns to shoot the audience with. """X it up!" Long Live Xerocracy!

SISYPHUS TIME

For Professor Heino Vanderjuice

I hurry to tell Dr. Blope that since *V* got pinched there are 33 references to idiots in Pynchon's latest *Against the Day*. I keep some things secret though. As any good mathematician who has aspirations beyond poetry I say to myself: at least 33 references. "Bloody idiots," Dr. Blope screams. He's not in the camp who joyously welcomes poets: "Oh my God! Another poet! How lucky we are!" He's with the masses who are exasperated: "you write poetry, get away creep." (These are actually Charles Simic's words, but as they say, you've got to steal from the best.) I tell Blope that I've just won the Pulitzer. "Have you now," he says, making a dismissive gesture. "You mean, theoretically?" he asks on second thought. "Of course theoretically," I say. "Anything else would be so boring." I want to imitate his rhetoric and say: "bloody idiot, do the math, man." While I go for nothing, I think of Zermelo's axiom of choice. "Have you told Vanderjuice?" he asks. "He's into that sort of thing." "Nope," I say. "He's stuck in the Michelson-Morley Experiment. Can't see nothing." You can't expect to see emotion in symmetry. And I hate symmetry. It only works in practice. "How do you feel, honey this and baby that?" In theory it screws up the smartest question: who the fuck cares?

"WHERE'ER WE TREAD 'TIS HAUNTED HOLY GROUND"

For Zarathustra

I think I look beautiful in my Lagerfeld creation of a white silk dress that goes all the way to the floor spilling over my brown Birkenstock trekking boots. I have a *rendez-vous* with Zarathustra on top of *Predikestolen*. He sees me from atop, waves at me and shouts: "you look like a parachute in all that mass of soft satin. Off somewhere?" He's jealous of my beauty. He's thinking of ways to possess it, but the whiteness blinds him. With his eyes closed he can't think properly. So it's very easy for me to just fuck him, and get it over with. But I have come for the natural solutions that lead to singularities. He wants gravity in vacuum. He speaks "Of the Virtue that Makes Small." I lose my native tongue, and start speaking in one I don't understand: *"Das Wandern" "Wohin?"* – *"Der Neugierige"* – by the time I get to – *"O Bächelein meiner Liebe,* how silent you are today" – oops, language is back – I see Jack Kerouac down on the road translating: *"Ungeduld"* – *"Dein ist mein Hertz,"* but then he also gets it mixed up: "Behold, think of Dean Moriarty!" "Did I say *Behold*, he asks, horrified? "Yes," I say. "That's Zarathustra's line," and then I explain: "when he's sexually frustrated he stops prophesying all that nonsense about unholy simplicity, and starts singing Schubert songs instead." I take off my dress, and all the men go: "*mein*, mine, *mein.*" I follow the gravity. The transvestites go with the vacuum.

THE H FUGUE

For Shulamith

– IN the *Hütte*, in the beautiful hair, in the garden, in the heart, in the hard, in the half – "This is compulsion," I tell myself. But I instantly make the realization that the best poetry around is the poetry that dares to aspirate its consonants. The diacritic for aspiration in the phonetic alphabet is the superscript "h", [ʰ]. Language in vacuum. I continue with my imaginary reading. In t[ʰ]e [ʰ]ouse „*dein goldenes Haar Margarete, dein aschenes Haar Sulamith*". Obviously Celan knew what he was doing – „*der Tod ist ein Meister.*" – "he grants us a grave in the air". In the [ʰ]air the breath is bereaved.

WHEN Eliza tried to learn aspiration she couldn't say: "In Hertford, Hereford and Hampshire, hurricanes hardly ever happen." This English Shulamith spoke no Hebrew. Cruel consonants are hard to caress. Hark! – Fight the snakes with your hair. Entangle their tails with your string, and drink, and drink, and then ding. The bell tolls for *der Tod*.

Aspire „*der Tod*", Shulamith, louder and more, and haunt, and let your hurricane happen — *in dein aschenes Haar* — Etch your Hs, imprint them on skin and let them burn it. It burns. The "Ah," loses its first born. The H remains and it haunts.

~~~

ABOUT THE AUTHOR

Camelia Elias is an associate professor of American Studies at Roskilde University. She has published academic work on the concept of the fragment, prose poetry, philosophy, feminism, psychoanalysis, cultural studies, queer studies, ethnic literatures, and visual arts.

Currently she is working on several book-length projects and on promoting American studies as visual studies across universities in Denmark.

www.ingramcontent.com/pod-product-compliance
Lightning Source LLC
Chambersburg PA
CBHW032011080426
42735CB00007B/575